FRACAS

F R A C A S

Paul Violi

Hanging Loose Press
Brooklyn, New York

Published by Hanging Loose Press, 231 Wyckoff Street, Brooklyn, NY 11217. All rights reserved. No part of this book may be reproduced without the publisher's written permission, except for brief quotations in reviews.

Printed in the United States of America
10 9 8 7 6 5 4 3 2 1

Acknowledgments: Some of these poems first appeared in *New American Writing, Upstart Literary Magazine, Nexus, Blade, House Organ, Log, Angle, Otis Rush, The World, Exquisite Corpse, Drainage Basin Artists' Alliance, The North, Sulfur, Free Lunch, Scratch, Jewels and Binoculars, Lingo,* and *Hanging Loose.* "Huggermugger" and "The Anamorphosis" previously appeared with drawings by Dale Devereux Barker in *Pataphysics Series No. 5.* "One Extreme to Another" was the text of "Jumbohemian 74," a collaboration with Barker and Chris Bloor. "Quick Sketch" was one of the broadsides in Louise Hamlin's *Bringing Up Baby.*

Hanging Loose Press thanks the Literature Program of the New York State Council on the Arts for a grant in support of the publication of this book.

Cover art by Dale Devereux Barker
Cover design by Caroline Drabik

Library of Congress Cataloging-in-Publication Data

Violi, Paul
      Fracas / Paul Violi
         p.   cm.
      ISBN 1-882413-63-6 -- ISBN 1-882413-62-8 (pbk.)
      I. Title.
   PS3572.I59F73   1998
   811'.54--dc21   98-42833
                                              CIP

Produced at The Print Center, Inc., 225 Varick St., New York, NY 10014, a non-profit facility for literary and arts-related publications. (212) 206-8465

C O N T E N T S

In memory of my father
Joseph Violi

The Anamorphosis

I

Now you are looking into the eyes of a man who woke up with an ear the size of a tuba. There's no telling how it happened. Fact is, he woke up that way, the strange effect of a lost cause. He thought he was dreaming at first, riding high dark seas on a half-deflated life-raft. But no, he lay sprawled on his own bed, clinging to his own ear, his tremendous ear.

With a pinch or two, a short slide along a decidedly auricular swirl, his fingertips confirmed it: the most remote, bloodless part of him, a lump of involuted insensitivity, had become the most—the ... most ... the *most* of him. He lay there listening to the sun rise, the darkness dwindle, the gentlest thing he'd ever heard. Water trickled, pipes trembled, the reheated house began to creak and stretch as if rising in his stead, high above him, while his great sponge of an ear continued to soak up his own being. Egads. Whatever could it mean? Another day, another undeserved problem. To one who has lived alone too long, life is especially treacherous.

What propels that whirling stillness in his eyes? Panic? That's one way of looking at it. A kind of sadness? ... Yes. Grief? Abandonment? Possibly. Medieval diagnoses tumble forth: his deformity is punitive, a pleasure-hound's comeuppance, Pinocchio's counter-charge, the result of being morally depraved or spiritually deprived. Or perhaps it's the effect of an overly solemn political view of art or an irredeemably comic awareness of his own condition. We can only wonder. At this moment, he simply recalls that the guardian of dreams had a brother, Momus, the god of ridicule. And, of course, that he's going to be late for work—again.

What else can rouse him to defy his fate? He does all he can do: he listens. He drools a little and listens. Car ignitions, the raggedy firing of untuned engines, the hum and flow of distant traffic, quickened footsteps from blocks away, stalwart citizens heading off to meaningful employment, the skirl of factory-whistle pipes: what he hears begins to sound heaven-sent, the music of prosperity, the promise of life-defining work calling to him—work and what begins to feel like salvation.

Can he sit up? No, but, by god, he tries. He twists himself half off the bed, kneeling, dragging his head along the mattress, and hoists himself up the bedpost. He tries to stand free, but unable to straighten his neck—so lopsided is he, his earlobe alone weighs more than a wet sandbag, a sack of chicken feed slung over his shoulder—he begins to totter and sway like a drunk on a tightrope. He crashes hard, the enormous plunger of an ear squashed, stuck to the cold floor. All he can do is stay there, sucking up a colder silence until all he can hear is his own heartbeat trapped—kathump-kathump-kathump—bouncing like wearied sonar off the earth's vast and empty core.

The blank of fatalism has refilled his eyes. But not for long. His ear has indeed shrunk a bit. Gradually, the suction relents and pops him to freedom. He embraces his ear and his fate and squeezes the weight out of both of them. As he compresses his ear, he can feel his determination swell like grandeur. He squirms across the floor and shoves himself through the door to daylight, to his job, his life's work, drawn by a music more powerful than gravity ...

II

It's The Science and Nature Section
and we're leaving.
No, it's The Sociology Section.
No matter, make a right.
Don't shove, don't push,
keep your place in line,
don't litter,
don't act silly,
and we'll be out of here
in a minute.

Don't throw anything.
Don't climb on anything.
And don't interrupt—I said
don't interrupt.

Stay in line.
How should I know what
A Bride of Quietness is?
Raise your hand.
No, that's a fruit bat.
No, I can't explain
the lascivious grin.
Yes, they're all depraved.
Next time, raise your hand.

No, we're not in the basement.
It's The Social Science Gallery.
Stop bouncing that ball.
Nobody buffs an armadillo.
They're born that way—smudge-free.

Don't touch.
Keep moving.
Yes, it looks like an attic.

Make a right.
No, we're not lost.
O.K. it is the basement.
Tie your shoelace.
Next corridor turn right.

Put that back.
This is not the attic.
I don't know the longest
one-syllable word in the language.

Keep going straight.
Yes, that is the longest
one-syllable word in the language.
Thank you!

We're not lost, we're back
in The Science and Nature Section.
Don't touch.
It's a portrait.
I don't know what it's doing here.
It's Stalin.
It says: "The muzhik
looked into his eyes and saw
the well where the devil drowned."
You don't know what a muzhik is?
Tough.

That's called a diorama.
How should I know?
Some kind of thatched
and tropical hebetude.
Does that help?
Too bad.
Don't touch.
Drop the bongo.

Keep up.
No stragglers.
Stay in line.
We're heading out.
Bejugglements coming up.
It's my word against yours,
and mine is bejugglement.

Stop singing, stop humming,
stop the yammering.
You want to boost a groundling?
You want heckfire and brimstone?
Blood and coal?
Theological, biological
and literary knickknacks?
You want feathered serpents
and spikey demons?
Then stop yammering.

No, read the caption:
It's an Etruscan hubcap.
That's a finch, the perky finch.
Yes, indeed, the seagull
is a songbird.

That's parchment, a bestiary.
You're supposed to guess:
"Born to bury himself all life long,
swelling the earth with his silence,
always seeking a darker blindness,
a deeper grave, the fearful—"
Give up?
It's Elmo the Mole!

Stop sniveling.
Keep moving.
We're not lost.

This might be The Art & Leisure Annex,
or it might be
The Social Science Gallery.
Who knows?
No, you can't take a nap.

I don't know what that means.
Try this one.
It's a prow, it's a Viking longboat,
It's killer elegance.
It's Svend, fork-bearded Svend
gazing fiercely into *Mare Tennebrosum*.
Does that help?

Then try this one.
It's a piece of something
by Bernard Palissy.
It says, "16th Century Ceramicist.
Burned down his own house
to keep his furnace going
just to finish it—whatever it was."

Let's keep moving.
No, it doesn't mean
whatever you want it to mean.
It's a flaming skeleton
racing across a field of daisies
and it means "Death of a Solipsist."

That's called
The Pleasure-hound's Lament.
The caption's in Latin.
It says, "My heart is a cliché
jammed inside a stale fortune cookie."

We're not lost.
No napping, keep moving.

That's right,
it's called *Love's Arrows*
Deflected by Chastity's Shield.

No, you can't take a nap.
Look at this one.
What do you see?
Another profoundly bamboozled visage?
You think so?

But step to the right,
way over, and look at it sideways.
Now what do you see?
A man with an ear the size of what?
A tuba? A coffee table?
Pretty interesting, huh?
Wake up! I said no napping.

Look, you know what a tableau is?
You know what sequins are?
You know what "bathos" means?
Well, after you've figured
this one out,
make a right, keep going
until you come to the sequined bathos
of Sweet Petunia
and Her Twinkling Hefties Quintet.
I'll be waiting for you.
Wake me up when you get there.

Bathos

One or two, it seems, turn up
each spring, not far off a road
where they'd wandered into the woods
until they dropped in the snow and froze,
providing filler for the local paper:
another middle-aged male,
unidentified, decomposed.

Reading about one of them yet again,
the usual list of what he wore,
how many shirts, pants, jackets,
socks, I find myself sliding back
into the same sad and hollow poem
I've tried to write before,
about how a person,
an all-American misfit,
moving from place
to place, job to job, can keep
putting on one self after another
without sloughing any off,
growing heavier but more hollow
with each menial part he has to play.

And so it goes, a half-formed poem
spun out of images of luck and loss,
rag and bone, soul and husk.
And when I think I'm at the point
where I can wrap it up in silences
that peel away, onion-like, or open
like a weak hand or, finally,
a mummy, empty, unraveling
as it's slowly twirled,
afloat amid dim stars and its own dust,
the poem stalls. I'm sidetracked again,
remembering myself, like so many others
who wandered around for a while

when young, in Afghanistan, in Nepal,
Turkey, Bulgaria, Spain,
getting dressed before going to sleep,
putting on all I had to ward off the cold.
I see myself again, in Amsterdam,
an impetuous kid on a Sunday morning,
April 9th, nineteen sixty-eight,
with a ticket home, a flight to catch,
but no money to pay the hotel bill.
How I got dressed again and again,
reluctant to leave anything behind, pulling
khaki pants over dungarees, tucking
flannel shirts under cotton shirts,
shoving a manuscript, a couple of years
of turgid poems, under my belt and,
finally, shoving myself into a blue suit
that'd been stuffed into a knapsack
for a couple of years. Sweating, barely
able to bend my knees or arms,
I lurch through the lobby, telling
the suspicious manager I'm off to church.

I try to hitchhike to the airport
but all I get are wary looks.
I still arrive early. Too early:
the check-in counter is closed.
Days without a meal, I want to be
first on line, first on the plane,
first seat from the galley.
Tired, woozy, I every so often
lean back to read the clock overhead.
I'm asleep on my feet, unaware
of the crowd forming behind me.
Again I open my eyes, lean back,
look up, but stumble, and as I feel
my shoe heel roll over something,
crush something soft but solid,
I hear a groan of agony

so profound my stomach knots up.
I turn in time to catch him as he falls.
His eyes squeezed tight, he tries to speak.
His eyebrows are slightly tweezed.
Tears run down his cheeks; his cheeks
are lightly powdered and rouged.
His hair, a shade darker than natural,
is finely cut and he's wearing
a long mink coat that matches his hair.
Trembling, crumbling, he leans on the man
next to him, also draped in mink
the same color as his dyed hair.
His face is powdered, too—It's Liberace?
Yes, it's Liberace and his friend!
I look down, we're all looking down
at his friend's foot, the shoeless one,
covered by a thick white sock.

Doubled over, he's trying to speak.
I try to pick up his cane
with my free hand, but packed
into my suit, poetry manuscript stiff
as a board against my stomach,
I can't stretch, can't reach it.
I'm afraid he's going to pass out.
Unbelievably, he attempts a joke:
   "Of all the gasp feet of all the toes gasp behind you gasp
you had to gasp step on the broken one! Unnnggnnhhgggh!"
   He slumps, collapses. A call for tickets makes the crowd
close in. I try to help, try to hold him upright while sputter-
ing apologies. But Liberace, looking at me, the way I'm mov-
ing, lurching backwards now, arms out-stretched, clearing
the way as we move along the corridor, my wrinkled suit
about to burst, tells me, very politely, very firmly, but with
something like dread rising in his voice, "Forget it, *please*. It's
nothing, nothing at all. I insist, really. I'm telling you: Will
you please stay the hell away from us!"

On an Acura Integra

Please think of this as not merely a piece
Of writing that anyone would fully
Appreciate, but as plain and simple
Words that attempt to arouse whatever
Appetencies you, especially, depend
Upon language to fulfill; that drench you
In several levels of meaning at once,
Rendering my presence superfluous.
In other words, welcome this as a poem,
Not merely a missive I've slowly composed
And tucked under your windshield wiper
So that these onlookers who saw me bash
In your fender will think I'm jotting down
The usual information and go away.

Overtime

Yet another Tiger Swallowtail
bounces around the phlox.
It doesn't look like a tiger anymore,
doesn't look much like a swallow.
It looks like a brand new
customized upholstery job
for a Cadillac convertible
owned by a platinum-blonde waitress,
heavy on the eye-liner,
who has to pull in a lot of
>   *How ya doin', honey?*
>   *What can I getcha, babe?*
overtime to make the payments.
So she's annoyed at the skinny guy
still sitting in booth ten.
He hasn't touched his order.
He's in a dither, he's stumped.
Scribbling, staring off, scribbling,
he's spinning his wheels:

>   Ah time, oh night, oh day
>   Ni nal ni na, na ni
>   Ni na ni na, ni na

He's lost the tune!

>   Oh life O death, O time
>   Time a di
>   Never Time
>   Ah time, a time O-time
>   Time!—

He tries again!

>   Oh, Time
>   O world! O life! O time!

He's almost got it!—

>   *Doncha wancha muffin, buster?*

20

Summer Reading Interrupted by Rain

... to think of the quality of life in the eighteenth century is inevitably, sooner or later, to think of Josiah Wedgwood's leg blip. Wedgwood, who was to trade and commerce in many ways what Samuel Johnson blip blip was to literature, was troubled in his younger days blot by some kind of circulatory complaint blip blip in one leg. If he happened to knock it against anything blot it swelled up and put him blip blip blippity blot in bed for a few days blot and since he was constantly blippity blip making journeys up and down England blippity blot in the course of building up his business blip blip he found the waste of time irritating blot blot blippity blot and had the leg amputated blot blot blip blip blippity blippity blippity blippity blot amputated without anesthetic blippity blot blippity blippity blippity blot blippity blippity blip

Mayhem with Dimwit

As soon as the patio was finished
they invited their parents
and cousins up for the weekend.
His father had a bad heart, very bad,
and he made weak jokes
   I'll take it anyway I can get it!
whenever they warned him to take it easy.
   Stop trimming those shrubs!
They thought he was joking at dinner
when he quietly laid his face
on the picnic table, but when he turned
blue and fell off the bench
they screamed and jumped, calling
neighbors to call the police.
They took turns giving him CPR,
took turns shouting advice
at whoever was giving it.
   Press harder! Pinch his nose!
In the middle of all this
   Didja get the ambulance?
the man who lives in the summer house
next door ambled down the road,
as he does the first day
he arrives every June,
to talk with each neighbor, one
at a time, in his loud,
onerously formal way.
Now he leaned over the hedge,
peered deeply into the mayhem and
   Hello there! What's new?
   How's every little thing?
At one point, the stricken man's
daughter-in-law, on her knees
beside him, looked up and around,
wondering if she could have

actually heard someone ask
> *You folks just up for the day?*
before a shudder of denial
ran up her spine and she was
swept back into the panic
> *My God! Where's the ambulance?*
> *Will ya try again, for Chrissake?*
> *Nice job you did on the patio.*
> *Do you hear any sirens yet?*
> *He's gone!*
> *I hope it stays like this all summer.*
> *No! Press harder!*
> *Did you buy that slate in Peekskill?*

One Summer Afternoon in the Back Bay

It was that second floor apartment,
corner of Commonwealth & Mass. Ave.
The cops burst in, guns drawn.
They leapt through doorways,
landing with legs spread, gun barrels
and eyes synchronized, scanning the rooms.
But it was the wrong place, a bum steer.
Even so, Fortin and whatever-his-name-was
refused to stop or acknowledge them.
The game was too close to call.
They had shoved the furniture aside,
taken the pictures off the wall
—converted the living room
into a handball court.
In shorts, sneakers, head-bands,
sweating like mad, they played
with a jaw-clenching intensity
that drew the cops over.
One looked at me, jutted his chin,
jerked his thumb toward the game.
I answered with a shrug, showed him
my hands, palm up, explanationless.
They holstered their pistols and watched
as serves were met with a dive, a leap,
a floor-slamming lunge that made
the tone arm bounce across "Rainy Day Woman".
It was ferocious, electrifying:
Swipe, snatch, skid, slap, whizzing arms
and volleys, flying sweat, muttered curses.
The cops were as captivated as I was,
the first time any of us had seen
the game played without a ball.
No-ball Handball: and yet not one point,
not one out-of-bounds call was disputed.
And when Fortin finally put

the game away, punched in a shot
that left what's-his-name
looking dumb and deflated,
he walked over dripping, breathless,
gave the invisible ball
one more sharp bounce off the floor,
and to welcome any post-game
commentary greeted the cops
with a triumphantly awshucks,
all-American-sportsman smile.
But the cops were already
backing out into the hallway,
the last one with his hands held chest high,
a wary pushing-off motion, a way
of saying Let's just ... Just ... Let's
just ... just ... Just let's ...

Tycho, Tyche ...

Tycho objected to Copernicus' theory
that placed the stars so far apart,
because he figured God
would not waste all that space.
And I sympathize with him
as I head down Third Avenue, figuring
that's the kind of incomprehension
that, along with the galaxy
of bottle-caps scattered
over the last intersection,
might eventually lead to a poem or two.
Countless bottle-caps dropped
haphazardly around a hot dog stand
over the years and pressed
into asphalt by car and bus tires
now look like a chance to find
and name, under the faded city night,
configurations as mundane
as goat and crab, dipper and fish.
So that's what I'm playing with
as I walk, space and waste and light
and chance, when, without making me
miss a step, this little black kid
sticks a gun against my heart,
another jabs one in my back
and a third rifles my pockets,
so cool and professional and polite
in their long black raincoats
and short-brimmed hats that
I'm frozen, speechless,
as they float me around the corner
and escort me into the shadows, saying
"This way, Mr. Charles."

Quick Sketch

Five years old, she inspects her new home.
She wants a yellow room, new friends.

She walks down the road,
wearing a bikini, high rubber boots
and a black lace shawl,
and introduces herself to the neighbors.

She asks me again, "What happened
to the dark stars?"
        I still don't know.

She says she has no idea
who trimmed the cat's whiskers.
She knows I don't believe her.

She says, "It's unfortunate
that god is invisible."
        I disagree.

She offers me another
butter-and-watermelon sandwich.

I say, "Sure. Pass the mustard."

Protracted Argumentation

As Voltaire advised, first define
crucial terms. Doing so often
obviates further disagreement ...

Nanosecond: the time the cab driver
behind you waits after the light turns
green before blasting his horn.

Clockwise: When you take the time
to get out of your car, walk back
to his, and ask just what it is
you could do to help him out.
Whatever he has in mind.
Clarify any problems with language,
verbal or gestural; provide
directions, literal or
metaphorical; or, in the interest
of fellowship, accept more
general inquiries on subjects
that concern or vex us all.
Propose the nature of time
itself as the perfect topic
to get things rolling again.
Suggest that the apparent crisis
become an opportunity to resolve
some of those paradoxes
that exasperate all who labor
under unrelenting urgency.
Point out that in order to cross
the intersection he must first
get halfway there, and to do that
he must get halfway to the half-
way point, and to do that he must

get halfway to the halfway point
to the halfway point, and so on.
So in fact he can never even start.
Suggest another, perhaps
equally enlightening point
of view: If he were to try
to catch up to you, he must
first reach the spot from where you
took off, and by then you
will have proceeded further,
and he'll have to reach that spot,
only to find you're still further
beyond him, etcetera, rendering
his efforts to overtake you
—even if you're turtling across
Canal Street—forever futile.
Consider that any consideration
of the indivisibly finite
and the infinitely divisible
will form a vise that will crush
the very life out of him right
then and there, unless you both
deal with the proposition
that since anything—say
a measly Honda or a flaming
yellow cab that appears to be
flying across an intersection
—any object, because it always
has to be occupying a space
equal to itself, can't be doing
that and moving simultaneously,
then the very idea
of motion is nullified.
Advise him that, consequently,
it makes no sense to compound
the illusion by pretending
to measure it with an arbitrary

system of numbers or colors,
these embellishments that are
supposed to remind us there's a time
to go and a time to beep,
when in truth the giver of warmth
and consolation, the sun,
is perishing at the very moment
you speak—if there is such
a thing as a moment.
The glorious sun a mere flicker
amidst flickering worlds, explain
how the end of all his imagining
is to see a sneaking suspicion
collide with a numbing certainty:
that beyond the blue afternoon sky,
beyond the darkness squeezing
the light out of puny stars,
lies a nothingness even that darkness
cannot fill, a destination
he can call transcendence,
if he still thinks there was
ever anything to transcend
to begin with, driving for all
he's worth into that blazing wisp
of his own extinction, knowing
it is the light he was born for,
it is regret he honks his horn for.

Paradox of the Somber Mountaineer

I got so good I could track it
over stone, surprised to find myself
still following the trail
by moonlight, by starlight,
over sand and ash and ice.

I could tell how far ahead of me
it was in the cold mud
by how much water had seeped
into the tracks, tracks so fresh
and sharp they could've been fossils,
could've been flowers cupping rain.

I could tell how close I was
by how much the wind had blurred,
or the melting snow dissolved them.
And comparing my own weight,
the depth of my own tracks,
I knew when it grew heavy
and weary, weak and thin.

And by the length of its stride
I knew as if listening to a heartbeat
where desperation quickened its pace
or where it dragged itself, senseless,
where it staggered and spun
in the morning light, finding
the trail looped back, knotted,
snagged and unravelled
again and again, smudged lines
in the brilliant grass
like something written with an eraser.

How close I was to it—I saw
where it brushed the dew off

saplings when it slipped back into
the woods—so close I thought there
was nothing more to know about loss.

Now how do I get out of here?

Complaint

They seem to know
this place
the way they step
so calmly into view

They must come here
often the birds
that bring
their best song to you

But the ones
that leave them here
unsung
and slink away

I think I was one
of them once
so long ago
maybe an hour ago

Not surly bright
but quiet
I was one of them
a nincompoop

Paleontologists
agree
at one time
nincompoops flew

But could they sing?
Yes
better than a goose
I think

They could sing
but Beauty
made them
dumb

Watching you turn
in candlelight
that's my best
my only guess

And when silences
gather in your eyes
like creatures
to a clear dark spring

in a clearing
where sunlight leans
its hazy beams
against a deeper blue

I see the face
of April in yours
so gay at times
it could be May

But then
when you turn
aside
when you turn

as austere
as autumn
so far away
almost solemn

I can't decide
With only
a simple flame
it's hard to say

With the colors
of this room drawn
from dark waters
colors that gleam

and slide over you
as light as honey
as dark as hesitant
as honey

With this bed as warm
as earth
that still holds
the heat of day

And nightfall
with all
its flags in my face
waving me on or away

And mornings
so soft and slow
you can hear a nincompoop
crow

I.Q.

Rolling brightly at my feet,
the same nickel
I just tipped the cabby.

*

Even the humble hoe
if stepped on the right way
—Stars in daylight!

*

Eight and two is ten.
Two from ten ... is eight.
But five and two is ... different.

*

Nail...thumbnail.
No wonder the hammer
often gets confused.

*

The trembling old clerk drops
coins into my trembling hand.
Call it change. Call me Palsy.

*

They'll return my clothes
if I pay for the mirrors?
Which restaurant left this message?

*

Hold the store door open
for the old man, he beats me
to the last paper. Prick.

One Extreme to Another

O Walrus, born to sleep,
        to flop on ice,
each a pillow for another,
send a benthic tune our way.
    Our heads feel like Calcutta.

Pour a brandy, swat a fish,
        flub and grunt,
    speak our languish.
Slumber's child,
    your buoyant tons
rise and fall
    like slumber's breath.
Nudge a rump
       and clack a tusk,
yawn and snap ... an azimuth.

Fall awake, wake to rest,
    slurp some slush,
       crush a mattress.
Through arctic nights,
       tumble and roar.
If it's furry, it's furniture.

Over ultima Thule,
       blink and doze,
lick a tongue, sniff a nose.
    Rumble and squish,
       grunt and snore,
but grant a wish to an omnivore.

O Walrus, maximum yawn,
    spare us one
       of your lullabies.
We've scribbled and drawn,
       dusk to dawn,
we're weary of truth and lies.

Synopsis: The Songs of the Jolly Flatboatmen

Row your boat gently.
You're headed downstream anyway.

Save your strength for the mudflats.

Never discourage merriment.

If anyone concludes that life
is but a dream and thinks
that's worth singing about
exuberantly, exultantly,
over and over again,
toss him overboard
into the maw of rock and ice,

and row on,
        gently, gently.

It will amaze you,
what you can get away with
and yet remain a jolly,
decent, generally compassionate,
semi-competent flatboatman.

Inscribed on the Gates to Canal Street

for Anthony Davies

Anthony, I wish you and Hogarth
and Doré, Daumier and Blake,
Rubens, Rembrandt, and Degas,
Currier and Ives and Ribera,
Whistler, Dürer, and Picasso,
Grosz, the Carracci brothers,
Rowlandson, Mantegna, Hokusai,
Corot, Manet, Piranesi and I
could hop into my Honda Civic
and drive back and forth
across Canal Street a few times.

We could jump in
the moment the steel window grates
are hoisted like floodgates
in the clattering dawn.

And when the merchandise,
hauled onto stoops and sidewalks,
begins to tumble like a riverbank
into the rushing day,
we could steer to and fro,
watching the tawdry and rare
collide, picking whatever we need
from the here and now,
the now and then,
for the rowdy allegory
the gates of this street deserve.

At least a few panels for each of us!
I already have one in mind:
the tour bus guide
with his bullhorn spiel:
"Forget the memorial plaque

in sedate cathedral corners, folks!
This is where New York
buries its jittery poets.

There's one, spiked head first,
with a store over him,
not a mere headstone,
to keep him down.
A legally designated landmark,
a pantechnicon,
windows loaded
with what was found
in his fathomless pockets."

And the store owners—
I love that look:
the noisy eyes
of race car drivers
who realize
they're taking tight turns
a little too fast.

And the signs—
Sea Quest Bicycles, Pearl Paint,
Angel Accessories and Angelo's Bar,
Taj Mahal Stereo,
Far Far Sports,
Queen Far Investments
and Burger King—the signs
mysteriously switched around,
the words reshuffled
every night, without confusing
anyone in the morning.

Certainly not me,
since the one that matters most
remains untouched, ubiquitous,
still sounding like something

out of Heraclitus:
"Everything Must Go!"

And so it does.
Some of it smack onto the gates
of memory and imagination.
There goes that blissful moron,
beaming up at the sun
while pissing like a horse
in the middle of the street.

And there he is again,
that middle-aged man,
impeccably dressed, more
than distraught, head bowed,
arms raised, fists clenched,
staggering along the sidewalk,
still pleading, still
demanding to know:
"God made everything else,
why not me?"

And there goes a group of students
to spend the day in a café
discussing higher mathematics
until a check arrives that
they can't divide with a hacksaw.

And here she is again,
that sad, weak, old woman,
all skin and bones, but
with such enormous breasts
—they weigh more
than the rest of her—she
has to lean on two canes
or else fall over.
Only this time I see
sullen, goofy multitudes

eventually falling in line
behind her, headed
for either the river of Forgetfulness
or Merciless Remembrance.

And again, some kid
wearing a bulldog collar
lets the pet rat on his shoulder
nibble his ear
while his girlfriend
selects another assassin figurine
for his charm bracelet.

And now a beggar walks off,
singing off-key,
sorting through the day's take,
tossing away the pennies.

And again, as a lady
passes me in the rain,
a spoke of her umbrella
hooks my right nostril
and turns me around
like a fool for beauty.

And again, behind a window sign
proclaiming Live Nude Dancers
(Why do they need
to specify "Live" ... ?)
two guys lean against the bar
and discuss the best way
to hunt bats:
    "Yuh gotta know what yuh doin'.
If yuh know what yuh doin',
yuh'll get yourself a 12-gauge."
    "12-gauge is only accurate for what?
for ... ten feet?"
    "Right. But yuh gotta know how to

attract 'em right."

"Best way I hear—"

"Best way is, throw stones over
your head."

"Huh?"

"I'm telling yuh, stones is best."

"Bat bait?"

"'Specially when it's dark. Darker
the better. Just toss 'em up and duck.
They'll go right for 'em. Yuh'll hear
'em flocking. Then yuh just hunch down
and pull the triggers."

"Simple as that?"

"It's all in the timing. Don't throw
them high enough, yuh get hit in the face.
Throw 'em too high, you're blasting rocks.
But if yuh don't keep tossing 'em up, the
bats bite your nose."

"Like anything else, I guess yuh have
to know what you're doin'..."

And there I am,
and here I go, on the street again
as the breeze off the Hudson
begins to gust, redolent
of something more exciting
than salt or money.

And as I step up to a pay phone
this brown-eyed girl
with a smile, a look that says
she knows there's no chance
I won't defer to her,
cuts right in front of me,
pushed a little by the wind.

And as she tries to speak
in the roaring air,

she watches me watching her
pull her long glistening hair
away from her lips and the phone,
and laughs when it's blown
back again and again.

And from a discarded cassette
near my feet, unwound tape
continues to slither
across the concrete.
Then it ascends, shimmering,
climbing the wind.
It flows and glides,
then it dips for a moment,
then takes off, snatched
by a cab antennae—the cab
she must have taken off in.

And as the cassette skitters by,
I pick it up, wondering
what the label says,
wanting to know what music
made the day take off like a kite,
pulling us with it—Liszt
and Bizet, Mendelssohn and Brahms,
Rossini, Schubert and Strauss,
Chopin and you and I.

Poem

after Gozzano

How strange ... to wake between

everything and
        nothing

and be able to make something

known as
        a paulviolipoem

Huggermugger

Ctesias:

The last enemies against whom Cyrus fought
were Scythians from Margiana, hoity-toity,
who were led by King Amoreaus, hot-shot.
These people, mounted on elephants, holy moly,
ambushed the Persians, helter skelter,
and put them to rout, higgledy-piggledy.
Cyrus himself fell from his horse, humpty-dumpty,
and a lance pierced his thigh: low-blow booboo.
Three days later, he died from the wound, loco.

Herodotus:

After decades of warfare, Cyrus, wheeler-dealer,
perished in combat against the armies, superduper,
of Queen Thomyris, hoochie-coochie,
who had long desired to avenge, rough stuff,
the death of her son, namby-pamby.
She ordered the body of Cyrus dragged, ragtag,
from beneath the slain and his head, harum-scarum,
thrown into a vat of blood. Jeepers creepers.
She then commanded the lifeless conqueror: "Drink
this blood, after which you ever thirsted, but
by which your thirst was never allayed, jelly belly!"

Xenophon:

Cyrus died tranquilly in his bed, fancy schmancy.
He had been forewarned in a dream, hocus pocus,
by a man with such a majestic bearing that he
appeared much more than mortal: razzle-dazzle.
"Prepare yourself," he told Cyrus, "for you will
soon be in the company of the gods, hobnob."

Cyrus, awoke and offered sacrifices, solo,
on a nearby mountaintop, sky-high,
not to implore the gods, hanky-panky,
to prolong his life, but to thank them, lovey dovey,
for their protection. Three days later, payday,
he gently breathed his last. Okeydokey.

Lucian:

Cyrus died of grief. Itsy-bitsy.
He was over one hundred years old, fuddy-duddy,
and he was inconsolable because his son, crumb-bum,
had killed most of his friends, brain drain.
But his son paid him all honors after his death,
building a tomb for him at Passagarda, grandstand,
a city Cyrus had built on the very spot, hot-spot,
where he had vanquished Astyages, who was none other
than his own grandfather. Wowie-zowie. Even-Steven.

Resolution

Whereas the porch screen sags from
the weight of flowers (impatiens) that grew
against it, then piles of wet leaves,
then drifted snow; and

Whereas, now rolled like absence in its
drooping length, a dim gold wave,
sundown's last, cast across a sea of clouds
and the floating year, almost reaches
the legs of the low-slung chair; and

Whereas between bent trees flies
and bees twirl above apples
and peaches fallen on blue gravel; and

Whereas yesterday's thunder shook blossoms
off laurel the day after they appeared; and

Whereas in the dust, the fine and perfect
dust of cat-paw prints scattered across
the gleaming car hood, something
softer than blossoms falls away,
something your lips left on mine; and

Whereas it's anyone's guess as to how long
it's been since a humid day sank so low,
so far from the present that missing
sensations or the sensation of something
missing have left impressions in the air,
the kind a head leaves on a pillow; and

Whereas the last of ancient, unconvincing
notions evaporate from the damp pages
of thick, old books that describe how,
for instance, Time and Love once

lay together here; how in a slurred flash
of light she turned and waded back
into the sea, and how the slack
part of any day was and is
all in the way he, half
asleep, felt her hand slip out of his; and

Whereas, the blue heron stands on the shore;
while the sleek heron turns, broad
to narrow, half hidden among the reeds;
turning with the stealth, the sweep
of twilight's narrowing minute,
of stillness taking aim; turning
until it almost disappears into
the arrowhead instant the day disappears,
until, staring out of the reeds,
the aforementioned heron
is more felt than seen; and

Whereas, you, with due forethought
and deliberation, bite into
an apple's heart and wish it were your own

On the Sly

Not blind to time,
       nor blinded by it,
Sit by my side
       and let the world slide.

Let the world slip,
       I'll not budge an inch.
Over the shrill echoes
       of the hollow earth,
Twenty caged nightingales sing:
          Let the world slide.
Though I have more feet than shoes,
       I have a lullaby.

Over shrill echoes
    of the hollow earth,
Call home your ancient thoughts
And fall into your dreams again.

Not blind to time,
       nor blinded by it,
Sleep by my side
       and let the world slide.
Let the world slip and slide.

Extenuating Circumstances

I don't know how fast I was going
but, even so, that's still
an intriguing question, officer,
and deserves a thoughtful response.
With the radio unfurling
Beethoven's Ode to Joy, you might
consider anything under 80 sacrilege.
Particularly on a parkway as lovely
as the one you're fortunate enough
to patrol—and patrol so diligently.
A loveliness that, if observed
at an appropriate rate of speed,
affords the kind of pleasure
which is in itself a reminder
of how civilization depends
on an assurance of order and measure,
and the devotion of someone
like yourself to help maintain it.
Yes, man the measurer!
The incorrigible measurer.
And admirably precise measurements
they are—Not, of course, as an end
in themselves but, lest we
forget, as a means to propel
us into the immeasurable,
where it would be anybody's guess how fast
the west wind was blowing
when it strummed a rainbow
and gave birth to Eros.
Never forget that a parkway
is a work of art, and the faster
one goes the greater the tribute
to its power of inspiration,
a lyrical propulsion that approaches
the spiritual and tempts—demands

the more intrepid of us
to take it from there.
That sense of the illimitable,
when we feel we are more the glory
than the jest or riddle of the world
—that's what kicked in, albeit
briefly, as I approached
the Croton Reservoir Bridge.
And on a night like this, starlight
reignited above a snowfall's last
flurry, cockeyed headlights scanning
the girders overhead, eggshell
snowcrust flying off the hood,
hatching me on the wing
like a song breaking through prose,
the kind I usually sing
through my nose:

> So much to love,
>   A bit less to scorn.
>   What have I done?
>   To what end was I born?
>
> To teach and delight.
>   Delight ... or offend.
>   Luck's been no lady,
>   Truth a sneaky friend.
>
> Got the heater on full blast,
>   Window jammed down,
>   Odometer busted,
>   Speedometer dead wrong:
> Can't tell how fast I'm going,
> Don't care how far I've gone.

The Hazards of Imagery

*The frescoes in the castle are by Pisano,
and they are so smooth and shining that
even today you can see your own reflection
in them.*

—The Anonimo

IN THE HOUSE OF MESSER SCONFORTO

In the solarium can be found
a famous representation
of giants in chiaroscuro,
singing and dancing
and tromping about the earth.
It is called Hymn to the Obvious.
It is a mysterious work,
an audible darkness,
and it is unforgivable.

In the sanctuary, to the right,
is an oil painting in which
Vitality is represented, wide-eyed
at the moment of waking, saluting
Death in the form of a toad
sitting on his belly.
It is an early example
of that type of brushwork
in which each stroke
is called a snarl.
Nevertheless, it, too,
is an unforgivable work,
scruffy and audacious,
cheerless and fireproof.

53

In the music room two busts
serve as a pair of bookends.
One portrays the young king
Mithridates
who, to make himself invulnerable
to assassins, sampled
poison every day; the other,
the old Mithridates,
who, when he desired to end
his life, could not find
a poison strong enough.
They are carved in stone.
Very hard stone.
But not that hard.

In the dining hall the group portrait
of a family weeping as they stand
over a puddle of milk
is by an unknown hand.
Many presume it is waterproof.
In fact, the application
of the slightest pressure reveals
it to be painted on an enormous sponge
that has recently been dunked.

In the mezzanine, Sprezzante
has painted The Great Cramp.
Is it Eternity, you ask, running
your fingertips across the cool wall,
or the loss of it?
Facing it is his masterpiece: The Shrug.

At the Palace of the Seccatore

The oil paintings in the stable,
depictions of Trojans trying not
to look a gift horse in the mouth;
of Agamemnon biting off more
than he can chew; of Nimrod
beating around a bush;
of Hector biting the dust
on the plains of Troy;
the study of Nessus giving
the wife of Hercules
the shirt off his back;
the one of Nausicaa
refusing to touch Ulysses
with a ten-foot pole: these
are all soggy and stale,
but the risk of contagion
poses an empty threat.
I should also note that the frames
are surprisingly sturdy.

The landscape on the stairwell
is by Capopietro.
It portrays the fieldworkers
of Pietrosanto, stout,
broad-belted folk
who leave no stone unturned.

The lavish silk tapestry
in the studiolo was executed
over the course of ten years
by Pringle of Gint
and it depicts
The Twelve Sultry Steps
to a More Powerful Vocabulary.
The figures it includes

defy description.
So delicately woven are they
their faces appear imbrued
with a glum and sickly light,
the porcine squint of hedonists
corrupted, I suppose, by a life
lacking any impetus save comfort
and ease, where even the most
shallow pleasure proves enervating.
Their eyes look like withered pearls
interred in rheumy oysters.
These faces leave me disturbed
and confused, and at a loss for words.

AT THE CHAPEL CARDINAL FINALE

Here is a painting on wood
by an unknown hand,
of hearty fishermen in an open boat
hauling a cow out of the Bay of Naples.
This painting smells:
an unfortunate odor no one
can eradicate or name.

Here, too, is a painting of the Savior
from whose eyes many have attested
they have seen real tears fall.
And I for one believe it to be so.
For I have heard this said
of other paintings
and recalling how they are all
so unbelievably bad,
so poorly executed,
I have concluded that it is
the painters' utter ineptitude
that has made their very subjects weep.
Such is the miraculous power of art.

At the Museum next to the Sign Factory

Not for impressionable souls, these paintings.
Some, like Sciamachy for the Marriage
of Empathy and Cynicism,
are so beguiling they make
people forget their own names.
Like chameleons, their complexions
take on the dominant hue
of whatever work they stand before.
A cheap trick if there ever was one.
A few of the painters
—irresponsible experimentalists,
neo-informalists, meretricious louts—
were captured and punished,
identified through the efforts
of a selfless investigator
whose own identity, sadly,
has been lost.

In the Gallery of the Repeat Offenders

On the stairway's second landing
one must confront a painting
called Feigned Injuries.
Bearing many illegible signatures,
it portrays a full orchestra
over which ragged birds
fly in a blinding fog.
At one time there were those
who extracted ready meaning
from this award-winning work;
to do so now, one
must take a plunger to it.
Which for a few small coins
an attendant will provide.

In the main room there is
a magnificent carpet,
very valuable, very skillfully
embroidered, whose theme
is The One Hundred Most Frequently
Mispelled Words in the Language.
The weavers labored in poor light,
praying to St. Eugene,
patron saint of spelling
and penmanship, for guidance.
Despite evidence of spurning
along the edges, and a few
scowls and slurs and scoffs,
and perhaps a little searing
and scuffing here and there,
and sloshes and slashes
and dibs, it shows
no signs of retaliation.

Here, too, hangs a series
of suspiciously pristine pictures
whose titles I will now record:
The Ascension of the Drudge,
The Forgiveness of the Drudge,
The Redemption—, The Descent—,
and The Agitation of the Drudge.
After viewing these pictures
for a while, I do not know who I am.
I cease to wonder about things.
I go to the piazza
where I feed the pigeons,
humming half-familiar tunes
as the heavens grow dim.

AT THE TOMB OF THE IMPROPERLY TRAINED BOMBARDIERS

This is the saddest work I have ever seen.
A tremendous concrete piano,
its maker unknown, yet
—O soul of man! unutterable sorrow!
Impenetrable silence!
The Great Echo!

The poems framed in the corridor
are by Maginot.
They are thick, the lines
impenetrable, true *vers Maginot,*
and visitors are advised
to simply go around them.

In the Gift Shop at the Lunatic Asylum

Always on sale, the figurines
of infants are made out of tar
and are produced by the inmates,
former apprentices
of Imbroglione, mostly.
On visiting days family
and friends purchase them
as presents for the inmates.

Here, too, Junior Achievers
can always join
the Aesthetics Club
and the Restoration Committee tours
that begin and end with the murals
of Mad Emmett, who even when
confined, isolated, deprived
of brush and palette,
continued to pursue
the beautiful, the ideal,
by painting the walls of his cell
with his own—his own—with his—
I dare not say what!

Near the Arsenal

In the gallery between the sanctuary
and the crater hangs yet another
scorched painting by Imbroglione.
This one from his series
The Perils of Tmesis
contains the confusing figure
of a deer in a garden
devouring four or five sythia
and two or three lips.
At first, specialists pronounced it
awe and then some; as did
the hot diggety dog common folk.
But when the Jesus H. Christ price
of the publicly commissioned work
became known, a great tintinnabululation
arose and a mob soon discovered
the picture was fool but not fireproof.

Next door is the museum
whose collection is devoted
solely to the heads
of very ancient statues.
And in the museum next to that,
in the most comprehensive display
of its kind, are the elbows.
And in the annex are the ankles.
And in The Great Shed, the knuckles.

UNDER THE BOARDWALK

Down by the sea
is a shop where one can purchase
an inflatable pope.
Inflatable saints, warriors,
luscious heroines and winged kings,
martyrs, triumphant crusaders,
and, for a slightly higher price,
the most inspiring philosophers
are also available.
Made by local artisans,
their features are truly lifelike,
truly cuddlesome, their sturdiness
and reliability guaranteed.
The people adore them.
They float on them in fountain pools
or moor them to their rooftops.
When strong winds blow
some choose to tie a bunch
of their favorites together
and grasping the lines as if holding
the most illustrious bouquet
the romance of history can offer,
they leap off the city walls.
Dangling from driven clouds,
they sail away, singing anthems
as they ascend, never caring
to come down to earth again.

AT THE PALACE OF MESSER MASSIMO

In the nursery the great canvas
that looms over the little cribs
and has as its subjects
The Modesty of Attila,
The Gumption of Achilles,
and famous conflagrations at sea,
is by Crassvoort of Holland.
The yellow smudge in the foreground
resembles a palm print,
but if viewed sideways
through a peephole in the frame,
it appears to be more than a smudge.
Not quite a swipe
but more like a smear.

The serene paintings opposite,
Infant Playing with Firearms
and Mother Spreading Butter on a Melon,
are, presumably, by that same artist.

The ceiling fresco looming
at an unfair height
over the dining room table,
a landscape that depicts mice
inspecting the skeleton
of an elk embedded in a frozen lake
is thought by many to be the work
of Crassvoort the Younger.

The painting of Cupid, asleep
on his feet in the infernal regions,
is very old, but as
it includes a pregnant mule,
a flounder, chicken lips,
a squirrel with a crazed grin,

and other such accessories,
it is thought to have been restored
in the studio of Crassvoort.
The canvas is loosely framed,
in the Northern manner,
to resist pokes and jabs.
And so it has, for the most part.

Over the River and Through the Woods

A well-worn path
leads to a quiet chapel
frequented by pilgrims
who venerate the ordinary.
From all walks of life they come,
their every manner and gesture
devoted to perpetuating the power
of the extremely familiar,
the predictable, the supreme
comfort of the commonplace.
So strong is their faith
that on these journeys
they continually flagellate themselves
with proverbs and platitudes,
vying with each other
in any situation to be the first
to utter the most amazing cliché.
Somehow they remain unscathed,
an effect noteworthy physicians
are at a loss to explain.
In the reliquary near the altar,
under thick glass, is the straw
that broke a camel's back.
And in another a golden egg
and a dead goose.

AT THE TOMB OF THE SEMI-FINALISTS

On the first landing is found a series
from the School of Imbroglione,
entitled The Exasperating Mysteries.
One, a manger scene, portrays
the figure of a babe
done in tar and honey.
Are tar and honey a reliable medium?
Should this painting be trusted?
Does it lack the depth
from which hope arises?
or is it, in fact, another
elevated argument
for the existence of the netherworld?
the goopy horrors below
this pleasant realm?

Another, to which I find myself
attached, noted for its technique,
for the determination
on the mother's face,
for the force with which she grasps
the basin, the sweep of her arms,
the wide-eyed flight of the babe
being expelled with the bath water,
—this one has been attributed
to the master himself.
All I can say with assurance
is that the frame
has been reinforced
and the work is impervious
to solvents or water,
whether splashed or soaked,
or, like the master himself,
sprayed with a high-pressure hose.

In the Municipal Workers' Garden

The numerous unfinished sculptures
are antique.
The tilted gazebo is antique.
The swarm of angels
attacking a malcontent is antique.

The slanted bench is a mistake.

The partially complete statues
along the trapezium
form a scene in which a few
human figures turn away in disgust
from something various gods
have gathered around and behold as marvelous:
an infant born with horns, hooves,
a smirk and a full beard.
These, too, are antique.

The sportive figures
of scantily clad crime fighters
are antique ... I think.

The caryatids that form
a complete catalogue
of job-related injuries—these
too, are all antique.
Perhaps the very work
that convinced Socrates,
son of a sculptor, to give up
training in that art
to become a philosopher.

A cooling blessedness,
an eye-filling dance of light
and shadow in water and air,

always rising, always falling,
water shadows, the undercurrent
of our own minds, replenishing bliss,
the invitation we've always sought
to play like a humming bird
in a great flower of water and light,
heart's ease in blooming stone:
all this the central fountain
would provide, if it worked.

Long-scheduled to be uprooted
the untended topiaries
have reverted into shapes
that are quite obscene.

Guidobaldo was the landscaper.
It was he who over a century ago
designed the undulant grounds,
scooped ponds and sand pools
out of the deep green lawn
and hither and yon dug
eighteen small holes
and inserted a cup in each one.
And the number eighteen
and the sand pools
have been much pondered,
but to this day no one knows why
he did such a thing.

The main structure
is The Apex of Disappointment,
an upside-down memorial
to disgruntled workers.
As for the unfinished busts,
the inattention to detail,
the way the tools left a profusion
of irks on rough or lambent stone,

these are the signature
of a sculptor known as The Chiseler.

The statue submerged in the pool
must be The Skeleton of Narcissus.
For unless I am mistaken
this is the very spot
where Narcissus first saw
his reflection and, horrified,
tried to strangle himself, fell
in the water and drowned.

AT THE MINISTRY OF COMMERCE

The enormous, jubilant work,
an altarpiece of sorts,
that celebrates
The Miracle of the Merchants,
the ones who succeeded,
with the application
of a barrel of oil,
in squeezing a camel
through the eye of a needle,
is thought to be a forgery.

The two-figured statue
in the foyer is,
notably, the only work
from the School of Trambusto
that contains decipherable captions.
That is, original captions,
not inscriptions added
later by enthusiastic observers.
The curiously appropriated figures
have been identified
as St. Augustine and St. Jerome.
The former explains: *Knowledge*
provides us with a basis
for comparison and judgement.
The latter concurs: *You ain't seen*
nothin' 'til ya seen
a dead whale on a flatcar.
The extended open right palms
of both figures, their
most prominent feature,
can hold candies or dry snacks,
monetary donations or soap.

Over the years reports
have stated that certain visitors,
supplicants from the ranks
of both high and low, some
so humble they didn't know
the names of their own fathers,
have stood before this statue
and been transported.
When they recovered
these visionaries found
they had experienced
an effect not unlike stigmata,
for their palms
were now smeared with grease.
Even more wondrous,
many witnesses to these events
have simply vanished.

IN THE BANCO GROSSO

Like many Romans
the ingenious Sprezzante,
the same who conceived
and designed the tollbooths
on the Via Dolorosa,
believed a tribute should display
the glory of the subject
without correcting his imperfections
or attempting to conceal them
from the eyes of the world.
Among his works here
is the snazzy life-like figure
of the surgeon Gianfrio,
who preferred to operate in the nude.
So tightly has the canvas
been stretched that the indignant,
the embittered, the vengeful,
are often re-injured
by the rebounding objects
they throw at it, and consequently
must be carried back to the hospital.

AT THE HOSPITAL

Trambusto made all these paintings.
He admired the light
in the operating room,
"the lustre of oblivion,"
and converted that place
into his studio.
It is said of him that he always
painted Oblivion the same way,
bristling with what appear
to be tears or sweat or
raindrops or Phoenix guano.

It is further said of him
that while preparing his studies
of obliteration he stocked
his kitchen pantry with samples
of soot and grime, cobwebs and dust.
That he tasted Oblivion
and pronounced it savory,
but, because it would never contain him,
giving off a whiff of disappointment.
It is agreed he was not a humble man,
and that with open arms,
as if trying to embrace
all he surveyed on his studio walls,
he often complained: *Where*
in the glare of eternity
is an eschatologist supposed to turn?

At the Guild Hall of the Ardent Miniaturists

The group show in the basement
consists of one painting,
a full frontal nude,
a majestic virgin
white as snowdrift.
It is a collaboration
from the busy little hands
of Giongolo, Cucciolo,
Mammolo, Eolo, Grumpy,
Sleepy, and Doc.

The facing wall appears bare
but is actually dotted
with tiny portraits in ink
that if viewed with a magnifying glass
reveal the faces of bloated biographers.
Selected for their ability
to turn the lives of the most
glorious artists into tales
of unrelieved pain and tribulation,
each biographer has been made
to resemble a flea.
For like fleas they thrive
when hastening an old dog's demise,
tormenting an artist
when he is weak and infirm.
And, after sucking his blood,
to allay their thirst
they hop into his eyes
and sip his tears.

AT THE GATEWAY TO THE PRISON CREMATORIUM

Above the entrance ramp,
the crystal and gold clock
bound with silver bands
engraved with mean-spirited tales
of beloved saints
was made by Milfred of Ulm,
yclept Milfred the Rat;
for like a rat, who must
constantly gnaw on things
to prevent its teeth
from growing so long
they would puncture its own brain,
he was considered congenitally,
incorrigibly, helplessly malicious.
According to signed testimony,
when he was a babe
his parents sold detailed prints
produced from the woodblocks
he was given to teethe on.
His work, considered
invulnerable,
was exhibited without reprisal.
At least in his lifetime.

In Villa Ferrara

Positioned above the balustrade
for all to behold hangs
the portrait of the gladsome duchess.
The work of the quick-handed Fra Pandolf,
commissioned by the duke himself,
this painting has been frequently nudged.
To my knowledge it is the first
to achieve a startling effect:
No matter where a viewer stands
the eyes of the duchess
seem to look everywhere
except directly at him.
While admiring Pandolf's ingenuity
the often and easily perplexed duke
questioned the significance
of certain background scenes.
Mainly, the priapic scarecrows
posted in distant gardens
and the figure of a gleeful nymph
astraddle a satyr,
holding on to his horns
while squatting in his lap.
Appreciative of Pandolf's
rendering of the duchess' wrist
and throat and jewelry,
the duke was particularly taken
with such details as her
finely fluted fingernails,
which indicated to him a diet
deficient in basic minerals,
especially zinc.

IN THE LOUNGE AT THE PHYSICIANS' GUILD

The standing nudes and odalisques
are by Pale Otis, The Swooner;
and his model was his beloved.
With her before him, at times
in a nightgown so sheer
she looked like a lily
afloat in a crystal vase,
he perfected that style
in which her limbs,
her munificent thighs,
are never outlined
but fluttered and rubbed,
gradations of light and dark
caressed to the drowsy transparency
of a pink flower
beneath the wings of a honey bee,
or a shoreline at high noon
to a wayworn sailor's eye.
He himself called it "strumming,"
drawing a plucked string,
the sweetest, most languid string
of the lute the moment before
it comes to rest, to show
how the sight of her
erased the line
between reason and rapture.

And he took care to preserve
these drawings with a fixative,
smudge-proof and fast-drying,
that did not alter his technique
or the texture of the paper;
that dried in seconds and caused
the least possible change
to delicate tints and values.

And he always tried to follow
directions, holding the can
at a 45-degree angle
12 to 14 inches above the drawing,
starting at the bottom, spraying
from side to side in overlapping
strokes as he proceeded to the top.

And this fixative contained ethanol,
methanol, and ethyl acetate.
And when he got some in his eyes
his assistants had to flush them
with water for fifteen minutes
and call for a noteworthy physician.
And when he inhaled it
his trusty assistants
would comfort his beloved
and call for a noteworthy physician
who would treat him
for injury to his blood
and kidneys and lungs.
And when he ingested it
he suffered confusion and headache,
instability and paralysis.
And to induce vomiting
his assistants would drag him
out into the yard and throw him
over the back of a mule,
then play cards in the shade
with his beloved and console her
until a noteworthy physician arrived
and a paler Otis was fully revived.

BETWEEN THE SHAMBLES AND THE BOTANICAL GARDENS

In the café many portraits cover the wall
behind the cash register.
They are not antique,
yet they are yellow, and they fizzle.
With their ice-tray grins
and bright eyes,
wildly inscribed salutations
and tributes and autographs,
the subjects must have been
famous recently: happy plunkers,
robust Thespians
and perhaps even minstrels
of great renown who sat
at the same table
as did the regular clientele,
singing songs, drinking drinks,
waiting for waiters.

Here, too, it was that Lorenzo,
Lorenzo the Pitiful,
with utter indifference
to his personal safety,
advanced the art of the place mat.
These are made of paper
and filled with illustrated,
informative tidbits whose purpose
was to distract waiting diners
from their powerful hunger.
Did you know that the eyes
of the owl do not move?
Did you know the giant tortoise,
with a lifespan of 150 years,
gets to wait longer
than any other animal?

Did you know that, according
to heretics, aimless mathematicians,
and those who study such things, this
dear earth's weight increases
by millions of tons a day
from the decayed skin
that each of us sheds
at the rate of three pounds per year?
Do you know why the eyes
of the owl do not move?
Do you, lovelorn, now
know the stare of the bereft?
Have you known all along
this dear earth was created
in an instant from nothing?
That each of us holds within us
a speck of that instant,
a craving void, a crumb
our hearts are supposed to feed on?
A pinhole a lifetime can not fill?
A seed of creation, out of which
the wilderness, where we pursue
greased pigs and immortality,
forever expands?
Did you know that oak tree
framed by the high window
before you never loses
all its leaves in the fall?
That I, a laurel gatherer,
have to climb its icy limbs
and tear the last of them down myself?
That they would hang there,
clumped, shriveled and whispering
through the coldest winter,
the wind twisting them into yet
another wreathe for Tithonus?
Waiter? Check please!
Waiter! Waiter!

At the Tavern of Messer Angelo on la Via Canale

The colossal nudes, Hercules
and Voluptuousness on a seesaw;
the mezzo-relievo of youths
who have wreathed their heads
in roses to cool their brains
while drinking wine;
the figure of the Queen
of the Goths bouncing
that of the God of Apology off a tree:
these are all antique.

On a large canvas in the hallway
is an altogether remarkable work:
Venus reclines in the golden arms
of common day, her eyelids a bit weary,
her glowing thighs as slick as wet clay.

Various silk tapestries
hang free from the rafters,
the work of an artist
who kept his eyes not solely
on man working in the dust,
nor on gods dreaming clouds on high,
but on the glowing rains
that hold them for an hour or so
in each other's thoughts.

One portrays Hermes, the glad god,
who moved faster than luck
or thought; who stole
what he could not himself create;
who first made music
—made it so effortlessly he seemed
to swipe it from the air—

and the first song he chose to sing
was a celebration of his own begetting.
(Trustworthy people have told me
that this work was filched
from The Tomb of the Secretary of Labor.)

Another, above the couch,
is said to represent
the devoted Lodovico, considering
the whorls of his lady's thumbprint
as a topographical map
of Mount Parnassus.

With the painting that shows Cupid
gazing into a mirror
that does not reflect his image,
Gaspari the Syrian poses
the question: When love can appear
so swiftly as to sneak up
on a mirror, how can mortals
and most gods defend themselves
against such a force?

AT THE COTTAGE OF MESSER VIOLI

The mailbox, painted dark blue,
sits atop a tilted cedar post.
It has a little red flag on one side
and it is altogether remarkable.

The Toyota in the driveway
is very old and is said
to have come from Japan.

There is in the hallway
an immense dogfood bowl.
It is made of iridescent pink plastic.
It is, as I have said, immense
and it is hideous.

In the kitchenette is a statuette
of Ceres, Goddess of Wheaties.

The dishwasher is a Kenmore
and altogether worthy of praise.

In the foyer the oversized painting
of a pork chop provides
visitors many opportunities
for conversation.

In the servants' quarters
there are many impressive works
that stress the imminence of death
and the probability of hellfire.

Placed on the broad maplewood table
beside bottles of cognac
there is a recording device
with a silver megaphone
into which natives may be
invited to shout
the oral histories of their people.

We, whose hearts have been gripped
by life, scoff at the idea of art
as mere ornamentation: So they
seem to proclaim,
the three statues that adorn
the neighbor's lawn, plaster deer
with real bullet holes in them.

Note: The unitalicized indented lines in "Overtime" are taken from the notebooks of Percy Bysshe Shelley. The paragraph interrupted by rain is from John Wain's *Life of Samuel Johnson*. Many phrases in "On The Sly" are from *The Taming of the Shrew*. The introductory quotation to the "The Hazards of Imagery" is from George C. Williamson's edition of *The Anonimo*, translated by Paolo Mussi.